Say the Word

Book of Poems

Reshonda Montreuil

published by IAmEncouragement, LLC
ISBN-13: 979-8-9891660-6-0

How Beautiful are You?

It's not just the walk and talk or overall appearance
It's the grace and gentleness that dwells within
The heart longs for attention
So I turn to worldly desires
When in fact someone is always attentive
But I lack discipline and consistency
Two things that can be acquired
I want to be beautiful not only in human eyes
But in the eyes of my Heavenly Father
Being seen elegantly and faithful
like a deer roaming the forest without a care or bother
I can't say I don't care what people think
When in fact I do sometimes
But what matters most is what Christ thinks
And that's to be whiter than snow
Without spot or wrinkle
Finding favor in his eyes
But true beauty isn't perfection
Perfection is a goal
Strive to be beautiful Man, Woman, Boy and Girl
Love is a start
Because he looks at the heart

Got a Minute?

Time is limited and life is short
There is a time for everything
So what is your time worth?
Time is the continuous progress of existence
It is the past and future
And let's not forget the present
Time is precious
And we say we don't have time for much
There is a time to be born and a time to die
Two significant moments if such
When is the Right time?
Is the real question
We go through life working and just rushing
It's not what they do to me, but what I do to them
Time is the same way
People lose it, abuse it
But it's really how's you use it in the very end
If you only had a minute
How would you spend it?

Living in Paradise

What does it mean to live in paradise?
Taking over the family business
Not worrying about clothes or food or any price
Now that's the life
But here's the thing, staying comes with a command
Love and show love
Without it, all that is left is an empty house
What does it mean to live in paradise?
Starting your own business
Trying to fit in, keeping up with trends
Thinking about every price
Trying to live the perfect life or just get by
All just to live by your own rules,
Do what you want to do.
But none of it matters you see
Either being and staying at home
Or leaving to find what you don't want
To realize where you're meant to be
Everyone could live in Paradise
It's for us all
And many are called
It's just some choose not to open the door
Or can't find it
If that's the case
Remember it's unlocked and available
You can reach it at your own pace
Don't let it be too late
So don't wait.

My Outfit

What am I going to wear today?
I usually wear something simple.
Jeans and shirt
But something always pops up that messes up the look
Like a pimple.
Nothing I can do about it;
Well, at least not right now.
Maybe my nice smile will cause it to be overlooked.
When I smile,I wonder why.
And so do you.
Are you just being polite?
Or are you happy too?
Either one is fine;
It doesn't mess up my day.
Some people get ready the day of,
But I got ready yesterday.
No time to rush, fuss, or cuss
Just want to be comfortable and at ease.
Then again choosing what to wear can be difficult,
For I dress according to how I feel.
So what's on display is not the clothes,
but the fruits that I bare,
For it's what's inside and outside that makes the outfit.
Being remembered for what I say and do,
Not just how I look,
But also how much I care.

Private Conversation

Free me from fear
For I don't want to feel like I'm hiding
Set me loose from eyes that may watch
It's not a secret
I just like my privacy
Hiding feels wrong
Yet everyone knows we talk
I just don't want to be interrupted in our dialogue
Why is that?
I ask myself, what does it matter?
I express my love to everyone else
But why is it hard to enjoy our chatter
When people are around
It must be fear
Embarrassed of what they may say
We should talk, cry, and love on you
Cherish you like you're our virtue
No matter any disapproval or accolade
You're just so special
And should be treated with care
I take our conversations personally
For it's not just words in the air
You listen and take everything in account
You talk back
Saying beautiful wonders
That I just don't want to miss out
So I'll continue to talk to you alone
For interference is a distraction
Thinking someone else is listening
The focus is gone
I rather have a private conversation

Mindless Idol

I'm bored out of my mind
There's nothing to do
Can't go anywhere or meet anybody
There's only surf the web and watch tv
Boredom is poison
Can I save myself?
How can I be saved if I'm the only one around?
Temptation lurks around like a shadow on the ground
For my body wants to do one thing but my mind knows
better
Obedience is better than sacrifice
I rather pray now than cry later
But what I have to do isn't always what I want to do
Some times I don't want to do anything
Then that's when something start creeping in
Boredom
What should I do?
What do I like to do?
What can I do right now, to end my boredom?
It's best to have a vision or plan for your life and work
towards contentment or success
If not, there will be many dry moments on your journey and
unnecessary stress
It's only boredom when there's nothing to do and you want to
do something
It's called relaxing when you've completed all that needs to be
done
Boredom is doing nothing by force
Relaxing it's doing nothing by choice
Which would you rather be?
It's all in how you use your time
There is always something to do
Pray without ceasing
Praise constantly
All to help not have an idle mind

What's your Story?

How should I write this story?
I hear planning is the way to go
Planning is helpful
But is that what makes the story flow?
Is it better to know or not?
Although neither matters
The story is a mystery
Full of suspense, like someone else is writing your script
The producer is important
But it's about the main character
And how they play the part
The actions of the person will show who's their director
And yes there will be mistakes
But I can't start over ,or stop half way
I can only write of the present
For it's full of surprises and convenient delays
That's what makes a story so great
Everything has its timing
It may not happen now
But it's never too late
The story I write is not for me it's for you
We help and need each other
To make our story a great one
Better than we can ever imagine

Fresh Air

Take a moment
Silence the mind
Close your eyes
See what you find
Search for peace
That pass all understanding
Focus on what you want
It's not challenging
We make it that way
Life brings stress
We forget that nothing matters
If not for happiness
So relax
Try to move onward
Never stop trying
And push if cornered
Take the Breath of Life, and live
A breath isn't complete until you Exhale
You can't breathe in forever
Some point you must let it out
And when you do just know it's more room for fresh air now.

What is Love?

The most precious things in life aren't things
It is the reason we breathe
One with breath could ever bring
It is pain and sorrow, yet beauty without limits
Joy, heat and passion
Traits it also exhibits
Reaching far and near,
Shown physically and emotionally
Also Spiritually, that goes without saying because it molded
me
Formed and shaped in your likeness
Only to gaze upon your true meaning
One of privilege should give, show and yearn
Because it is the souls purpose of living
Love is its naming.

Why?

A one word question often asked
Three letters that weigh such a mass
I see no need for it, but some may contrast
'Cause everything happens for a reason and that's a fact.
Many people cry "Why me?" as a first task
Why don't things go right?
Why can't I do this?
Wanting the problem to pass
But the truth is that our troubles won't last
It's not about the why, but the Trust and its' vast.
It's nothing wrong with asking why
For it shows your interest to know more
But when Faith is involved,
that's a time where we shouldn't have to ask
Why?

Decisions Decisions Decisions

There is no middle
There will always be consequences
It's a personal action
Either That or This
My dear brothers and sisters
Take note of this
Be slow to speak and and slow to become angry,
And everyone should be quick to listen.
Choose Hope
It's just like saying maybe
Its not a yes or a no
It's a possibility
A great one in fact
For it leans towards your favor
But if not now, it must be later
So go through the Test
For it leads to strength
Strength causes Success
Then Success creates Confidence
It's all up to you
The ball is in your court
Choosing is a gesture of free will
You may be knee deep
but there is always a way out and abort
Leaving doesn't mean loss
For there is always a better way
Choose life Get another chance to get it right
Make your Choice
And have your Say.

That "Something"

Something told be to look first
Something said go back and check
I should have followed my first mind
Ever wonder what that "something" is?
It's always right
But majority of the time we don't listen
That "something" speaks to all of us
Some choose to listen
It's not your fault if you don't
You're just not familiar with his voice
That "something" is always with us and will never forsake us
So cast your anxiety on him, for he cares for us
And if you hear his voice don't harden your heart inside
How would you know it's his voice?
You may ask
It's within, it's acceptance only self can recognize
That "something" loves you and wants the best for you
That "something" is Christ our Lord and savor speaking to
you.

Mankind in Reality

Fear is uncertainty
Anger is a monopoly
Sadness is our epiphany
Love is "The" epitome
And we all are trying to live in harmony
It's complex yet intriguing
It's weak yet powerful
It's a human yet a vessel
Doubtful, worried, confused
What's to make of it?
You weren't made that way
You were made in his image
The image of Love, Joy and Peace
The perfect image to say the least
Imagine how great it'll be to be free
Be your true self, who you're suppose to be
Full of Light and Life
Doing only what you can do
Belief is Optimistic
Striving is our logic
Caring does magic
Living is Epic

If Only...

If there's a will, there's a way
If only I knew what to say
If I should travel where would I go
If I be FaithFull then dreams will follow
If I seized the moment
If I pause in thought, efforts could plummet
If I be a good spouse, a good parent
If I'm a good friend, a good example that is apparent
If I do what I love
If I love what I do far above
If could be a word of the past and future
If is merely a possibility
If could bring about a change
If use correctly

A Good Song

It's not about the melody or tempo
It's not really about the lyrics
It's about how it's sung
We all went to grade school
We all had a dream or goal
But how can your song be sung if never told
We are all different
And nobody is perfect
The best part of life is when you realize your purpose
What I am suppose to do
What I like to do
What I am good at doing
Three things that can counter each other
But have one common answer
The more challenging it is the better the song
It's no better satisfaction than over coming something
difficult
The feel of relief of getting it right all the way through
Making no mistakes
Doing it perfect is possible but after many takes

Self-Love: Growth

Can I miss what I never had?
Can I show it, if I don't have it?
Can I find it, if I don't know what I'm looking for?
Can I accept it, if never taught acceptance?
Can I live happy, if I'm not happy within?
Can I be of benefit as I am now?
We ask ourselves questions to bring awareness and growth
Learning about ourselves can produce maturity, and unveil
our self-loath
It's all to do better and be better in the Present
So in the end we can hear, " Well done my good and faithful
servant".

Be Encouraged

Think on things that are pure and lovely,
Stay positive and productive around people that are bubbly.
For there is always good in a situation,
And that good is that the problem won't last
So don't beat yourself up because things aren't going in the
right direction
There is one goal despite the many paths.
Then again a great way to feel better is to cry out in your
secret closet.
Write it down and get it out
Moving up and forward is the objective
No time to ponder and wonder
For life is short
It's either take it or leave it and being selective
There's a time to be happy and a time to be sad.
Embrace all the motions and accept that things will happen
And it's only for a moment which isn't bad. Words have
power
The power is in our tongue
It is because we say it is
And if we believe it, then it's done.
Look up and be encouraged
Father, Mother, Daughter, and Son

Faith vs Knowledge

You won't know when you're ready. It's a leap of faith
Things have to happen to make us stronger
They happen to build character
If we knew the future the present would be no longer

Getting your hopes up is having faith
For it's the anticipation of success
But faith drops when a plan B exists

Knowledge is like saying "it can happen"
Faith is like saying "it will happen"
The difference is the certainty of something
There is doubt in knowledge because there is a chance of
failure
Whereas there is only belief in faith because it's the
Substance of things hoped for, and the Evidence of things not
seen
There is no in between

Knowledge can only take us so far
It's taught
Faith is experienced
Knowledge is natural
But faith is supernatural

We can't depend on our own knowledge and understanding
For it's not always what it seems
Faith displays what the eyes can't see
It creates and fulfill dreams

Slow Motion

I'm moving in slow motion
Can't gain momentum
What's going on?
Maybe I'm afraid of being told no so I'm being extra cautious
But I'm moving in slow motion
And can't gain momentum
What's going on?
Maybe I'm afraid of hurting someone's feelings so I'm careful
in what I say
I'm moving in really slow motion
And can't gain momentum
What's going on?
Maybe I'm being inconsistent in my work
Things aren't slowing me down
I'm slowing myself down
With all the distractions, temptations, contemplations
Will I ever speed up?
What am I to do?
I guess I'm can be grateful that I'm moving at all
At least I'm not standing still and have no clue
The race isn't given to the swift
But the one who endures to the end
So I can't lose
No matter how slow I'm going
I will work on my craft diligently
I may not see how it'll work but I'll work on my craft to
increase my faith that it'll come to pass
Faith without works is dead
Walk by faith not by sight
That's better done than said

A Never Ending Job

In all honesty we are all children
We are always learning, and growing
We fall, and make mistakes
No one is perfect or all knowing

But there's one someone
Who I don't mind modeling
One who has sufficient grace
One who gives new mercy every morning
One who doesn't spare the rod

It's all for the betterment of the person
To save them from death
Parenting can be challenging
But parents are the teachers of the earth

That's why it takes a village to help groom the kids for society
The village are the people who have walked, talked, and
experienced life
Their stories help make our stories great

All in all we are suppose to help one another
For the times are changing
And a new era has already begun

So I guess a parent's job is never done

Forgiveness

Being common isn't common
No one thinks the same
That's why the world is fascinating
But it's complicated when someone complain

Common courtesy, Be polite, Treat others they way you want
to be treated
Are all famous sayings
But what's the difference between venting and complaining
It's the goal of forgiveness
Even though it's not easy
Letting go is more rewarding than saying your feelings
Let's be seen as the bigger person
And become blameless and pure
Not speaking ill of anyone
For letting life take its course is the cure
Forgetting is forgiving
No grudges to hold
And love so deep that it's blinding
Over looking all the wrong
Lastly don't take it out on them
For it's not them
We wrestle not against flesh and blood
But against spiritual forces of evil
So Live, Love, Give
And try to Forgive

Discipline

We go through life thinking challenges come to give us a hard
time
We do get experience from hard ship but there's more to gain
We get a testimony
A reward for making it through
Some stuff is worth the pain
He discipline those he loves
The hurt isn't for nothing
It's a sign that he's paying attention and hasn't forgotten
So count it all joy
He won't put more on us than we can bare of one something
It's all so we can fulfill our purpose
Trails come to make us and mold us to the people we need to
be
Creating strength, perseverance, and opened eyes to see
How humans are weak
The need for greater help is found with humility
So we can be truly happy
Discipline is healthy

Obsessed

What happens to the eager enjoyment after experiencing
something you've always wanted?

I always thought that once you get it, then I should be happy
When in fact it was only joy for a moment

I asked for God to satisfy me so I won't have to look for any
other satisfaction
Then I thought aren't I suppose to be satisfying him?
It goes both ways.
If we keep the zeal and fire alive to want to know him more
He'll give more of himself to us, if we open the door

The excitement is Faith
Since we don't know what'll happen
If we're working hard on our dreams
All we can do is trust that things will work out
It's such an adrenaline rush
Especially if your trying BIG things

Once you get obsessed with the possibilities using Faith
The thirst for more of Christ is indefinite

Limits

Do you have a limit?
Should there be a limit?
Limit on love
Limit on patience
Limit on time
How to take the limits off is the real question
Limits off of Self
Is it possible?
Is dreaming a crime?
Society has shaped our line of thinking
Money gets you higher
When in fact our attitude is our altitude
It's the way we see things and the thought process that
makes a good fighter
The thought of knowing it'll happen, but don't know when
Patience is challenging
It's what to do until then?
We mustn't get weary in well doing
But be of good courage and strong
Think on things above
And put the limits on high so all options and possibilities are
known
Then there's nothing wrong with reaching your limit
For it's the realization for need of greater help
So if we reach our limit in every area to achieve
Let's be limitless in faith
Because all things are possible to them that believe

Relationships

We freely choose to be with someone
It's not for what they have or can give
It's the potential of great love and having a companion
But even in a relationship
There are rules
It's not for restriction but respect

He loves us
He respect us enough to let us choose
No pressure is applied
That's the true meaning of free will
There is nothing to loose

Love is blinding
When we deeply love someone
We always go back
We overlook many mistakes
We'll do anything it takes

That's how he sees us and can give grace and show mercy
But no one wants a one sided relationship
The things we do for love
It's all done in our own leisure
Out of our own interest
All to live happily ever after

Religion is rules
Christ is Relationship
He knows all we know and have learned
The Word tells us how to love him in return

For more Books/Journals

visit:

www.IAmEncouragement.com

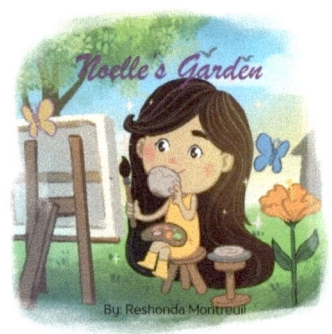